FOREWORD

In 1978, the FIP Commission on Practical Construction decided to form a working group with the title Maintenance, repair and strengthening of concrete structures. Dr N. Petersons was the Chairman of the Group and the members were Messrs D. J. Boot, J. D. Crawley, M. A. G. Duncan, W. D. Handley, P. Mohr, L. Muehe, P. H. Perkins, R. L. Preston, J. R. Ridings, G. Ruffert, J. D. W. Shaw, B. Westerberg and C. Zavliaris.

When a draft report was presented to the Commission in 1982, the Commission decided that it should be divided into two reports: one on inspection and maintenance; and a second on repair and strengthening.

Dr Petersons resigned as Chairman in 1982 and the present Guide to Good Practice was produced by an editorial group headed by Mr W. Bilger. The guide is an updated version of FIP Report 15.383, which was published in 1978.

In the last three decades a vast number of structures have been built, representing a huge investment. It is now recognized that reinforced and prestressed concrete structures need to be maintained in order to preserve their structural integrity and, therefore, their economic value.

This guide includes very valuable information on inspection and maintenance and I wish to thank the editorial group, under the chairmanship of Mr Bilger, for its excellent work.

P. Matt
Chairman

CONTENTS

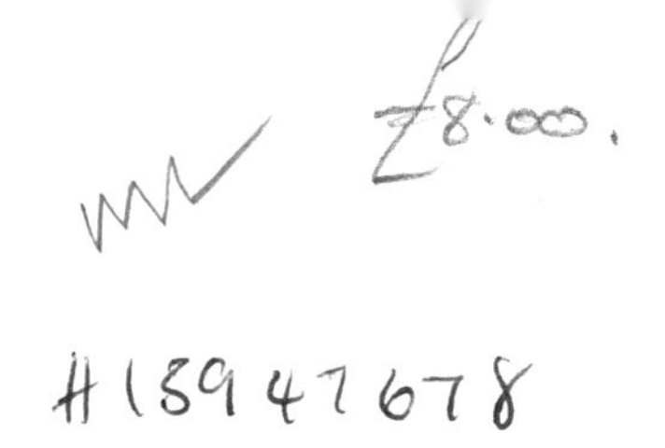

einforced
oncrete

FIP COMMISSION ON PRACTICAL CONSTRUCTION

Chairman: P. Matt, Switzerland *Technical Secretary:* W. E. Murphy

Members

M. Adam, France
M. Banic, Yugoslavia
W. Bilger, West Germany
P. Boitel, France
Cheng Qinggua, China
B. D. Cox, South Africa
M. Ducommun, Canada
S. P. Fadon, Spain
I. Fogarasi, Hungary
J. v. Geest, The Netherlands
J. Groenveld, The Netherlands
S. Inomata, Japan
R. W. Irwin, New Zealand
P. J. Jagus, India
D. Jungwirth, West Germany
J. L. Koch, Australia
Å. Lindblad, Sweden
J. Lindgren, Norway
G. S. Littlejohn, UK
P. Mohr, Denmark
L. Muehe, West Germany
N. Petersons, Sweden
W. Podolny, USA
J. J. Sarrang, Hungary
H. D. Starke, East Germany
T. N. Subba Rao, India
J. Torvinen, Finland
K. L. J. Trinh, France
G. Via, Italy
B. Voves, Czechoslovakia
E. Woelfel, West Germany

Editorial Group on Inspection and Maintenance of Structures

Chairman: W. Bilger, West Germany

Members

W. E. Murphy, UK
J. Reidinger, West Germany

Published by Thomas Telford Ltd, Telford House, PO Box 101, 26–34 Old Street, London EC1P IJH, England

First published 1986

ISBN 0 7277 0261 0

Set by Bell and Bain Ltd, Glasgow

Printed and bound by Echo Press (1983) Ltd, Loughborough and London

1. INTRODUCTION

Concrete load-bearing structures are subjected in use to many types of environmental influence—or even attack—and it is therefore of great economic importance to prevent their deterioration. To keep the structures in a good state they have to be inspected regularly—and maintained. When designing concrete structures it is important to consider the requirements for proper inspection and maintenance, i.e., access, necessary facilities, etc.

This Guide to Good Practice deals mainly with inspection, which is a major part of preventive maintenance. However, maintenance is a much wider topic than is covered in the present guide, and attention is therefore drawn to the very large number of publications that are available and, in particular, to the *FIP Guide to good practice for the repair and strengthening of concrete structures.*[1]

Maintenance comprises any work, including inspection, necessary for a structure to continue functioning as intended, or to sustain its original or required standard of appearance. Preventive maintenance is any work necessary to prevent a structure deteriorating to such a degree that its function will be impaired, or to prevent more extensive maintenance becoming necessary.

Inspection of existing structures is the process by which any deterioration in the structure is observed and recorded. It comprises any work undertaken to determine and assess the condition of the structure, including the collection of information detailing the development of any deterioration.

2. IMPORTANCE OF MAINTENANCE

In general, concrete structures require little maintenance other than inspection and minor repairs shown to be necessary as a result of inspection. However, in some instances cleaning is necessary because of environmental pollution, industrial deposits, plant growth, bird droppings, nests, etc., and is particularly important where the accumulation of debris might prevent the movement of expansion joints or bearings. It is also necessary to clean drainage systems regularly to avoid problems from ponding of water or build up of water pressure.

Failure to maintain a structure may have the following consequences.

(*a*) The appearance of the structure may deteriorate.
(*b*) There may be deformation or cracking, causing concern to users or people in the vicinity.
(*c*) Costly or extensive work may be required at a later date, or premature replacement may be needed.
(*d*) The load-carrying capacity may be reduced, with consequent risk of ultimate failure.
(*e*) The structure may become unsafe for both the user and people in the vicinity.
(*f*) The structure may be reduced in value.

The main reasons for maintenance and inspection are

(*a*) to control the functional requirements and provide assurance that the structure is safe and fit for its designated use
(*b*) to identify actual and potential sources of trouble and misuse at the earliest possible stage, and to prevent serious deterioration and failure, consequently increasing the service life
(*c*) to monitor the influence of the environment since there is a relation between the aggressiveness of the environment and the durability of concrete structures; the increasing content of aggressive agents in the atmosphere, acid rain and the use of de-icing salts considerably diminish the life expectancy of concrete structures
(*d*) to provide feedback of information for designers, constructors and owners on the factors governing maintenance problems, to which necessary attention is best paid during the design and construction stages
(*e*) to provide information on which decisions concerning preventive measures and work can be made; it is cheaper to repair minor damage at an early stage than to replace major components or the total structure in the event of failure.

3. INSPECTION OF EXISTING STRUCTURES

It is vital for the results of all inspections and maintenance work to be accurately and fully recorded, including nil returns, so that a complete history of the structure is readily available at any time. During and following inspections it should be remembered that any deterioration has a cause, and it should be the aim of the engineer to determine the cause. If the cause is ignored, the deterioration will be repeated. The as-built working drawings, design calculations, soil reports, etc. should be available to assist in the assessment of the need for maintenance, the diagnosis of faults and any reassessment of load-carrying capacity. Where there are statutory requirements regarding the inspection and maintenance of structures by either the owners or a statutory authority, these should be incorporated in the inspection programme.

3.1. Inspection classes

Inspection can be categorized into three classes: routine, extended and special inspection. Besides categorized inspections there are casual and cursory observations made by users of the structure or people who happen to be in the vicinity. These are unlikely to be made at regular intervals but can be of major importance.

3.1.1. Routine inspection

A routine inspection should be carried out methodically at regular intervals. The inspector should work through a checklist which has been jointly prepared for the particular type of structure by the engineers responsible for both design and maintenance. The inspection should be carried out by a trained inspector under the general supervision of an engineer and the results compared with the results of previous inspections. A written report should be made of the condition of the structure and its various parts. The routine inspection is primarily a visual inspection and, in general, special access, plant or equipment are not necessary.

3.1.2. Extended inspection

An extended inspection should be carried out in place of, let us say, every second routine inspection. The aim of an extended inspection should be to carry out a close and more intensive examination of all elements of the structure, and thus special access, remote viewing techniques, underwater equipment, and so on may be required. If this is unacceptable, representative sections of the structure should be closely inspected. In addition to the checklist of the routine inspection, special instructions applicable to the structure in question have to be considered. A full written report containing photographs and drawings should be prepared, where necessary.

It is recommended that routine and extended inspections should be carried out by the same person(s).

3.1.3. Special inspection

A special inspection is made in unusual circumstances where for example

(*a*) a specific condition is discovered by casual or cursory observation or by a routine or extended inspection
(*b*) specific conditions are found for similar materials or similar structures, e.g. concern over the condition of concrete containing high-alumina cement in certain structures resulted ir the close inspection of many other structures
(*c*) structures are subjected to critical stresses or ar known to have weaknesses, e.g. a highwa bridge before, during and after the passage of a exceptional load
(*d*) subsidence occurs in areas of mineral or coa extraction
(*e*) settlement may become greater than tha allowed for in the design
(*f*) exceptional events (e.g. flood, fire, collision, etc. occur
(*g*) seismic activity takes place
(*h*) scouring takes place
(*i*) there is change of use of a structure.

The special inspection may require a great deal c supplementary testing and structural analysis and ma even include research.

3.2. Inspection intervals

Inspection intervals are a matter for engineerin judgement and must be decided for each situatior They depend on many factors including

(*a*) the type and importance of the structure
(*b*) the loading conditions and the severity c loading
(*c*) the consequences of failure
(*d*) the presence of an aggressive environment th influences the speed of deterioration
(*e*) history
(*f*) economics.

Table 1 gives a general indication of the interva that might be applicable for routine and extende inspection.

Structures are classified 1, 2 or 3 as follows

Class 1 where possible failure would have catastroph consequences and/or where the serviceability of th structure is of vital importance to the community
Class 2 where possible failure might cost lives and/o where the serviceability of the structure is c considerable importance
Class 3 where it is unlikely that possible failur would lead to fatal consequences and/or where period with the structure out of service could b tolerated.

Environmental and loading conditions are defined a follows

(*a*) Very severe: the environment is aggressive an there is cyclic or fatigue loading

Table 1. Indication of inspection intervals (in years)

Environmental and loading conditions	Classes of structure					
	1		2		3	
	Routine inspection	Extended inspection	Routine inspection	Extended inspection	Routine inspection	Extended inspection
Very severe	2*	2	6*	6	10*	10
Severe	6*	6	10*	10	10	—
Normal	10*	10	10	—	Only superficial inspections	

*Midway between extended inspections.

(*b*) Severe: the environment is aggressive, with static loading, or the environment is normal, with cyclic or fatigue loading
(*c*) Normal: the environment is normal, with static loading.

It is possible that the consequences of failure may vary from one part of a structure to another; hence one part of a structure may be classified differently from another. Similarly, the environment or loading conditions are likely to vary within a structure. Hence, different parts of a structure may need to be inspected at different intervals.

3.3. Signs and causes of deterioration in concrete structures

The reasons for deterioration are either physical or chemical processes which cause visible signs of damage. Inspectors should therefore look in particular for the following signs of deterioration.

3.3.1. Spalling

This is caused by, for example

(*a*) the corrosion of steel reinforcement or other embedded metal
(*b*) the freezing of cracked or porous concrete
(*c*) chemical attack
(*d*) poor quality concrete
(*e*) insufficient reinforcement or overloading
(*f*) thermal shock due to fire or fire-fighting activities
(*g*) accidental mechanical damage
(*h*) bearing of a concrete member on another with insufficient joint width or with joints choked
(*i*) the bearing area being too close to the edge or end of a concrete member.

3.3.2. Cracking

Cracks in concrete do not always jeopardize the safety or bearing capacity of a structure. The possible effects of cracks must be considered in the context of cause, location, statical system and environment and utilization of the structure. Cracks may be the cause or effect of a fault or both. Reinforced concrete is not wholly monolithic.

The design and structural analysis of a reinforced concrete structure are based on the hypothesis that the concrete will crack in the tension zone before the reinforcement bars can take up the tension. Cracks in this part of a member will therefore not directly affect the immediate loadbearing capacity of the member even if the cracks are of considerable width. However, cracks in the concrete cover will permit the entry of corrosion-accelerating agents to the steel, and thus break down the corrosion protection of the reinforcement. Consideration should therefore be given to the possible need to seal by injection cracks that are wider than those allowed by the building code.

Consideration may have to be given to the fact that cracks influence the stiffness and dynamic response of a structure, where this has not already been considered in the design. Unforeseen cracks in prestressed structures may entail a risk of fatigue failure, if they are subjected to repeated loading.

Cracks in the compression zone of a loadbearing member are often indicative of a lack of shear resistance, which could lead to ultimate failure of the structure.

Cracks can be classified on different bases. A simple method is to classify according to the primary cause as follows.

Cracks in fresh concrete. These can be caused by: plastic settlement (slump cracking); plastic shrinkage; form movement; or heat curing.

Thermal cracks. These are: cracks across the whole section caused by heat of hydration; surface cracks caused by heat of hydration; or cracks across the whole section caused by the influence of ambient temperature.

Shrinkage cracks. These can be due to: restraint from the surrounding structural elements; drying from one surface; different shrinkage rates or times; or different total shrinkage.

Durability cracks. These can be caused by: freezing and thawing; corrosion of steel; attack by sulphates; or aggregate reactions (e.g. alkali–silica).

Cracks caused by loading. These can be due to: bending; tension; shear; torsion; bond failure; or concentrated load.

Other cracks. These can be due to: fire damage; overloading; settlement; incorrect prestressing; impact; or secondary effects of tendon curvature.

Before a repair method is selected the cause of the cracks must be determined. It is also necessary to determine whether the cracks are active or dormant. The behaviour of a crack is checked by means of periodic observations utilizing tell-tales.

An acceptable crack width is dependent on functional requirements and the cause of cracking. National design codes usually limit crack widths. The values are admissible limits for theoretically calculated crack widths and differ considerably from those observed on actual structures.

3.3.3. Debonding of joints

This is particularly liable to occur where there is a large change in cross-sectional area or where dissimilar materials are bonded to concrete; for example

(*a*) at epoxy resin expansion joint nosings
(*b*) where mastic asphalt waterproofing material is used
(*c*) where there is a thin topping layer such as granolithic flooring
(*d*) where sealants are used.

3.3.4. Erosion

Mechanical action due to usage, weather and water leads to abrasive wear caused by sliding, scraping and/or percussion. The erosion caused by a jet of water with very high velocity may even involve the same mechanism as cavitation.

3.3.5. Corrosion of concrete through chemical attack

The highly alkaline cement-paste formed by the hydration is subjected to chemical attack, which can only act through dissolution in the pore water of the cement-paste. The resistance of concrete to chemical attack depends therefore on the water permeability of concrete, on the type and size of the pore system, and on the type of cement used.

Attack in the form of dissolution. Easily soluble compounds can be washed out of concrete or cement-paste by the continuous access of water.

Attack in the form of expansion. Heavy soluble compounds remain within the cement-paste as they recrystallize in the capillary pore system. If they then occupy more space than in the original form, expansive stresses occur which may lead to bursting of the structure of the cement-paste.

Attack by dissolution, as well as by expansion, may also occur in certain types of aggregate. Some agents deleterious to concrete may be harmful even in low concentrations when present in flowing water and brought continuously to the surface of the concrete. If the same agents are present in the mixing water they are often harmless, as the chemical reactions have often terminated before the concrete hardens, so that no subsequent deterioration occurs.

Chemical or electrochemical attack. This may be caused by: acids; sulphates; alkalis; alkali–silica reaction; alkali–carbonate reaction; organic and inorganic salts; soft water; aggressive gases; or electrochemical attack (due to stray currents).

3.3.6. Sagging of beams and floors, bowing or inclination of columns and walls, opening or closing of joints

These may be caused by: settlement; overloading; deterioration or failure of the concrete, reinforcement or tendons (due to stress-corrosion cracking and hydrogen embrittlement); or the conversion of high-alumina cement.

3.3.7. Excessive efflorescence, discolouration or staining

Reasons for this may be that chemical attack may have taken place; salts may be present in the concrete constituents; the concrete is porous, allowing the passage of water; the conversion of high-alumina cement may have taken place; the concrete cover is too small or the concrete may be permeable (showing rust stains); the ducts of tendons were incompletely grouted (showing cracks and rust stains).

3.3.8. Damage caused by vibration

Vibration seldom causes problems with concrete structures, but checks may be necessary where heavy industrial processes are being carried out.

3.3.9. Faults in design, material and workmanship

Faults in design, material and workmanship may increase the risks of excessive deterioration as described above. Thorough investigation of the statical calculation and drawings may show whether a structural component has reserves or whether it needs to be strengthened or repaired.

Faults in design include poor detailing; reducing the dimensions of the concrete members below the minimum permitted by the code (i.e. architectural aspects); inadequate concrete cover; errors in calculation and human incompetence (resulting in an inadequate safety factor); incorrect design consideration of tendon curvature and/or structural curvature; the complex interaction of numerous parameters for impact and impulse loading and difficulty in predicting the structural response to these loads; inadequate assessment of the construction stages and temporary scaffolding and formwork.

Faults in materials include poor quality or use of the incorrect type of: cement; aggregate; admixture; or water (i.e. chloride, sulphate, or sugar content).

Faults in workmanship may occur during the following processes

(*a*) storage of materials
(*b*) installation of scaffolding and formwork
(*c*) batching: in particular, the addition of excess water, in order to make placing and compaction easier, may reduce the strength of the concrete and increase its permeability
(*d*) mixing: in particular, mixing time may be inadequate
(*e*) compaction: this may result in honeycombed patches and low strength
(*f*) placing reinforcement: this may result in cracks, reduced bearing capacity or, more frequently, inadequate cover
(*g*) curing: cracks may be caused through early shrinkage and increased concrete permeability, thus reducing the protection provided to the reinforcement.

3.4 Assessment of existing structures

The stability and durability of a concrete structure can only be guaranteed where it has an appropriate safety margin against expected forces and environmental influences during its intended lifetime. To assess deterioration in a concrete structure an inspection is needed—in serious cases involving testing by special techniques.

3.4.1. Preliminary assessment

Safety factors in building codes are usually chosen to minimize the risk of brittle failure. In practice, therefore, most failures will be preceded by a warning in the form of large deflexions and extensive cracking. Where the strength of a structural element is endangered by some deterioration or damage there will normally be time for a preliminary assessment of the need for strengthening.

Initially, the structural drawings should be studied to determine whether the building component in question is loadbearing. A quick study of drawings and calculations together with an in situ inspection are generally sufficient to determine whether the structural component has been overloaded or whether reserves are still available. Where necessary, immediate measures should be taken to effect the final strengthening or repair work.

3.4.2. Final assessment

The final structural assessment should include a careful inspection using techniques appropriate to the kind of deterioration or damage. The objective of the assessment is to estimate the residual strength of the structure in order to decide

(*a*) whether the residual strength or stiffness of the structure is sufficient to assure an adequate safety margin, not only for use under normal conditions but also for other exceptional events that may arise, such as fire, earthquake or impact
(*b*) whether measures need to be taken to obtain a suitable level of safety for the structure.

Since all structural inadequacies that adversely affect strength or serviceability arise from

(*a*) deficiencies within the structure (i.e. faults in design, material or workmanship)
(*b*) changes in external circumstances, e.g. environmental influences, abnormal loads, fire, resulting in excessive demands on the structure

a systematic approach to structural assessment must include the following.

Visual inspection of the structure. This should be carried out in order to detect all symptoms of damage and defects, and should include a check on the actual dimensions of the structural elements concerned.

Study of existing documents. This should include a study of codes, structural analyses, drawings, specifications, soil investigations, the construction diary, previous inspection reports and everything relevant to quality control, design and construction of the structure.

Estimation of loads. Loads should be estimated to compare the actual loads and the settlement or rotations of the foundations with the assumptions of the structural analysis. For prestressed structures the conformity of structural analysis, drawings, actual stressing forces and the effects of concrete shrinkage and creep should be checked.

Consideration of environmental influences. These include aggressive agents in the atmosphere and rain, temperature, and the use of de-icing salt.

Determination of material properties of steel and concrete. Several inspection techniques and types of equipment are available for the determination of material properties and for structural assessment.

3.5. Test methods

The techniques and equipment should be selected in relation to the class of inspection (see Section 3.1), the faults recorded, and the extent of the deterioration or damage. Good access is needed for carrying out inspection works.

In general, routine inspections rely mainly on visual assessment using standard tools and methods, whereas extended and special inspections are also supported by more advanced tools, methods, techniques and equipment. The accuracy and limitations of the instruments and techniques should be ascertained. Advanced instruments and methods require a higher degree of engineering knowledge and training and possibly a high degree of comprehensive experience.

3.5.1. Standard inspection tools

These include the following

(*a*) clipboards, chalk, markers, clamps, etc.
(*b*) tapes, folding rules, callipers, sounding line, feeler gauges, paint-film gauges
(*c*) straight edge, level, plumb-bob, protractor
(*d*) thermometers
(*e*) inspection mirror, binocular, magnifying glass, camera, flash light, crack microscope
(*f*) pocket knife, wire brush, scraper, pick, shovel
(*g*) screwdrivers, pliers, hammers, torque wrench
(*h*) corrosion meter, increment borer.

3.5.2. Advanced instruments and techniques

Non-destructive and partially destructive methods. A rebound hammer (the Schmidt-hammer) and Windsor Probe are used for the cursory assessment of concrete strength.

Sounding is used to detect and locate fractures or concrete lamination under the surface.

An ultrasonic technique is used for

(*a*) assessing the homogeneity of concrete
(*b*) determining the location of possible defects such as foreign substances, cracks (which may also be hidden) and areas of low density
(*c*) determining the thickness of concrete members where there is access to only one face
(*d*) determining the dynamic modulus of elasticity
(*e*) assessing concrete strength.

A cover meter (magnetic detector) is used for

(*a*) measuring concrete cover
(*b*) detecting reinforcement bars
(*c*) determining bar size and direction.

An acoustic crack detector (based on ultrasonic pulse echo techniques) and magnetic crack definer (based on magnetic field disturbance techniques) are used to detect and define cracks.

A dye penetration and magnetic particle technique is used in the detection of cracks.

Radiography (X-ray or gamma-ray) is used for

(*a*) defining cracks
(*b*) determining the quality of concrete, e.g. its homogeneity or the presence of cracks
(*c*) checking the location and condition of reinforcing bars or prestressing tendons (e.g. for errors in positioning, abnormal deformation, steel failures and fractures, corrosion or lack of bond)
(*d*) checking the quality of grouting
(*e*) determining the approximate density of concrete.

Electrical half-cell potential measurements are used for indicating the extent of corrosion of reinforcing steel (but not to determine the rate or amount of corrosion).

Inductive magnetic measurement is used for detecting steel failures and for checking the corrosion and deterioration of reinforcing and prestressing steel.

A technique of acoustic spying, where acoustic sounds are received and recorded, is used for the detection of failures in cables, ropes, prestressing wires, strands or bars.

Dynamic testing using an electro-dynamic vibrator is carried out to check stiffness, continuity and possible defects in piles.

Endoscope inspection and a vacuum test are used to check small, inaccessible cavities (ungrouted ducts, for example).

Wet chemical analysis is carried out to determine the total proportion of chloride present in a normal Portland cement concrete.

Nautical and diving instruments, soundings, underwater cameras and underwater television cameras are used for assessing structures under water.

Paint-film gauge and radiometric devices (using beta or gamma rays) are employed for measuring the thickness of coatings.

Electrical resistance measurements are taken to assess the effectiveness of waterproofing membranes where the membrane is a dielectric material.

A tensile strength test (using a steel plate glued to the concrete surface) is used to determine the tensile strength of a concrete surface area before work begins on shotcreting, coating or sealing with steel sheets.

Surveying instruments are used for measuring various kinds of movement.

Inductive transducers are used with corresponding recording devices to take long- and short-term measurements of various kinds of movement.

Strain gauges, mechanical and mechanical–optical instruments are used for strain measurements and for calculating the corresponding stresses.

The Barkhausen-effect is used to check the residual stresses on structural steel parts.

A hardness meter is used to distinguish mild steel from high yield reinforcement.

Electrical measurement techniques are used for the assessment of dynamic properties, i.e. the measurement of frequencies and amplitudes.

Mechanical devices, pressure transducers, load cells and hydraulic pressure devices are used for the measurement of forces and pressures.

Load tests are used where there is doubt concerning the serviceability of structural members. The structural strength investigation performed by structural analysis can be confirmed or replaced by load tests. The resulting reactions (e.g. deflexions) of a structure can give valuable information on overall behaviour.

Since any particular method of assessing the condition of concrete from one mechanical or physical characteristic is only approximate, it is advisable to use a combination of non-destructive tests, each measuring a different characteristic, and to compare the results.

Destructive methods. There are two main destructive methods: core cutting and destructive load testing. Core cutting is the most direct method of ascertaining the strength of concrete in a structure, and is the testing of core cylinders drilled from the structure.

The samples should be taken in an area which is as representative as possible of the most critical concrete zones. Coring through prestressing cables must be avoided. Each estimate of characteristic strength should be based on at least nine test specimens and a mean value should be based on at least three test specimens.

In addition to tests on the strength of specimens, tests can be carried out for the determination of

(*a*) homogeneity of the concrete
(*b*) porosity
(*c*) air content
(*d*) frost resistance
(*e*) the type and grading of aggregates
(*f*) cement content
(*g*) depth of possible carbonation
(*h*) possible evidence of chemical attack
(*i*) the presence of chlorides and their concentration
(*j*) the presence of sulphates
(*k*) organic pollution in aggregates and water
(*l*) pH value
(*m*) the presence of blast-furnace slag in the cement.

The normal way to test the quality of steel is to cut off a piece of steel and examine it in the laboratory.

A destructive load test (leading to failure of the member) applied on a definite area, split by cuts from the whole structure, gives direct information on the actual load-bearing capacity of the member (i.e. the limit state).

3.6. Interpretation of results

When an assessment has been made of the condition of the structure, the observations made during the inspection should be evaluated. The result may be that defects are minor in nature and can be easily remedied, or are obviously not detrimental to the safety of the structure.

The defects or deterioration may, however, be such as to affect detrimentally the function of the structure as a whole. The remedial measures required in this case may involve extensive rehabilitation.

It may be necessary to place restrictions on the loads. It is important that the required remedies are made in due time.

4. INSPECTION OF STRENGTHENING AND REPAIR WORK

Since strengthening and repair work differs from normal construction practice and is very often carried out with unconventional methods and materials, the quality control of the work in progress and of the final product requires careful inspection by experienced engineers, to ensure that the properties are in accordance with the preliminary tests or assessments that have been the basis for the design of strengthening and repair.

As far as possible the quality of the final product should be controlled by the use of established testing methods published in the national standards, but there are other possibilities for an experienced inspector, as follows.

It is recommended that he should

(*a*) inspect the quality of the surface preparation produced by hammering, grit blasting, flame cleaning, etc.
(*b*) check that all carbonated concrete surrounding the reinforcement, and all poor concrete, has been removed
(*c*) check that prestressing and reinforcing steel are free from harmful corrosion
(*d*) test the quality of sprayed concrete (for compressive strength, bond between layers, bond between the sprayed concrete and the substrata and homogeneity) by cores drilled out; the bond should be tested approximately four weeks after work has been carried out—this can be done by light tapping with a hammer

(*e*) ensure that the quality of grouting material is as given in the specification

(*f*) ensure that for epoxy mortar and resin injections the handling procedures given in the product literature are followed; record weather conditions and temperatures while work is in progress; and thoroughly check the preparation and cleanliness of surfaces before placement.

Feedback of information on the cause of deterioration or damage, the long-term behaviour of concrete structures, and the suitability of the different methods of strengthening and repair will add to the existing knowledge on reinforced and prestressed concrete structures. All written reports on the analysis of deterioration or damage, all work statements and quality control reports should therefore be recorded. The documents will be useful for the improvement of national standards and will serve as examples of possible solutions in similar cases.

REFERENCE

1. *The repair and strengthening of concrete structures. FIP Guide to Good Practice, to be published.*